PICTURE SORTING

Written by
Sue Lewis and Amy Stern

D1254206

Editors: Carla Hamaguchi and LaDawn Walter
Illustrator: Darcy Tom
Designer: Carrie Carter
Cover Designer: Barbara Peterson
Art Director: Tom Cochrane
Project Director: Carolea Williams

Table of Contents

Picture Cards

Beginning Consonants

Beginning Consonant Blends

Beginning Consonant Digraphs

Ending Consonants

Short Vowels

Long Vowels

Rhyming Words

Syllables

Sorting Labels

Beginning Consonants

Beginning Consonant Blends

Ending Consonants

Vowels and Syllables

Sorting Mats

2-Column

3-Column

4-Column

Introduction

Sorting is a valuable activity in word study. Sorting activities are highly effective in teaching children to find patterns that make decoding easier. A picture sort is an activity that requires children to group words into different categories. This draws their attention to phonemes or word patterns and helps them make generalizations about how words work. These sorts are helpful tools for developing phonological awareness in emergent readers.

Everything you need to introduce sorting to your children is here in this handy resource! You'll find pre-made picture cards, sorting labels, and sorting mats to guide children through the sorting process, as well as a variety of activity ideas. Picture sorting is easy to integrate into your curriculum because all the materials are provided and the sorts do not require much direct teaching. Just punch out the cards and you're ready to go! Have children participate in a closed sort to teach and/or assess a particular concept or an open sort to allow children to determine the ways in which certain words are categorized.

Extend children's learning by having them write the name of each picture on one of the reproducible sorting mats. Children will make a connection between spoken sounds and their corresponding letters or letter groups. These simple sorting activities can supply the missing link that your children need to "crack the code" of written language.

The sorting activities can be used for whole-class instruction, individual work, cooperative groups, learning centers, and parent involvement. So wait no longer; start picture sorting today! Engage children in learning as they explore words and phonemes through hands-on experiences and learn how words truly work!

Getting Started

In order for children to have a firm grasp of the concept of sorting, it is important to provide them with many opportunities to practice sorting other materials, such as buttons, pattern blocks, or seashells, before you begin the picture sort program. Once children are familiar with the concept of sorting, choose a picture sort appropriate for your children's skill level.

1 Prepare Materials

Picture Cards—Pull apart the cards, and laminate them for durability. Place each set of cards in a resealable plastic bag. Write the name of the activity (e.g., Beginning Consonants) on the bag with a permanent marker.

Sorting Labels—Pull apart the sorting labels, and place each set of labels with the corresponding cards. The cards and labels in each set are color-coded for easy reference.

Sorting Mats—Pull out the sorting mats, and laminate them for durability.

2 Explain Sorting Rules

Decide whether the sorting will take place in a small-group setting, a large-group setting, in student pairs, at a learning center, or individually. Explain to children which type of sort they will be completing. It is usually best to start with an **open sort**. The goal of an open sort is to have children figure out a sorting pattern themselves. Have children look at the picture cards. Encourage them to find some type of similarity among the pictures to determine how they are going to sort the cards (e.g., ending sounds, beginning sounds, counting the number of letters in each word). Then, invite children to sort the picture cards and describe their sorting method. Allow children to sort the cards in any way they choose as long as they can justify their choice.

Once children are comfortable with open sorts, move on to the more advanced process of a **closed sort**. The goal of a closed sort is for children to complete a specific sorting pattern that has been predetermined. When children complete a closed picture sort, ask them to spread out the picture cards in front of them. Have children look at the picture cards. Ask leading questions such as *What sound do you hear at the beginning of most of these pictures? What vowel sound do you hear in these pictures?* Do not specifically tell children how to sort the picture cards; rather, guide them to the specific type of sort being completed. Then, invite children to place each picture card below the appropriate label on their sorting mat.

3 Create a Sorting Workspace

Children will use the labels to customize the sorting mats. Give a child or group of children a bag of cards and labels and a sorting mat that corresponds with what they are sorting. For example, if children are sorting all of the syllable cards, give them a 4-column mat. Children will place each of the four syllable labels (*1 syllable, 2 syllables, 3 syllables, 4 syllables*) in a column of their mat. Then, they will sort the picture cards on their mat.

The cards and labels can be used on any surface. You do not need to have children sort on a mat. Give each child a large piece of construction paper, and have children draw lines to create a sorting mat. Or, have children use yarn to create lines on their desk to create a sorting board. Sorting can also be simply done by grouping the labels and pictures into separate piles.

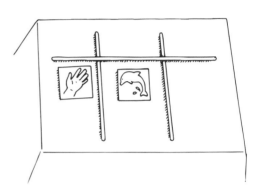

4 Record Answers

After children have completed a sorting activity, give them a copy of one or more of the reproducible sorting mats (see pages 9–12). Have them label each column and write the name of each picture in the correct column. The words are provided on all of the cards (except the rhyming and syllable cards) so emergent writers/readers can simply copy the word and fill in the missing letter(s). Use the answer key (pages 7–8) to check children's answers.

4 Column Sorting Mat

cK	d	f	g
duck	bird	leaf	leg
truck	toad	roof	dog
			pig

5 Follow-Up

After the class has finished a category, hang a sheet of chart paper in the classroom. Write the category and sorting rule(s) at the top of the chart. Then, invite children to write words or draw pictures of new words that fit the pattern rule as they come across the words in their daily reading and writing.

Teacher Tips

Variations

Each of the sorting activities has a set of cards and corresponding labels. A few of the activities vary slightly in their format.

The **Beginning Consonant Sort** has beginning consonant letter cards instead of labels. Have children place the letter cards in a row on a table or on the floor. Then, have them sort the picture cards and place each card under the appropriate letter.

The **Beginning Consonant Digraphs Sort** has the digraph cards on the same page as the picture cards. These digraph cards (*sh, th, ch, wh*) can be used as the sorting labels.

The **Rhyming Sort** does not have any labels. Have children place rhyming word cards in pairs.

More Sorting Ideas

There are several ways to have children sort the picture cards. The following are some additional sorting ideas.

Short or Long Vowel Sort

Give children a 2-column sorting mat and some of the short and long vowel cards. Have children sort the cards into two groups (short vowels and long vowels) on the mat.

Speed Sorts

Time each child as he or she completes one of the sorting activities. For fun the child can keep track of his or her time and repeat the sort to try to complete it in a shorter time.

Number of Phonemes

Give children a set of picture cards. Have them sort the cards by the number of phonemes (sounds) in each word.

Picture Card Inventory/Answer Key

 **Beginning Consonants**

b—book, bottle, bow
c—car, candy
d—door, dinosaur
f—fan, fork
g—girl, guitar
h—hippopotamus, hand, horse
j—jet, jeep, jacket
k—kangaroo, key
l—lettuce, lion
m—milk, monkey
n—necklace, net
p—parachute, pencil, pizza
q—quilt, question mark
r—robot, rainbow
s—scissors, seven
t—telephone, turtle
v—vase, vacuum, violin
w—watch, window
x—x-ray
y—yo-yo, yarn, yawn
z—zebra, zoo, zero

Beginning Consonant Blends

bl—block, blanket
br—bread, brush
cl—clothes, clown
cr—crown, crayon
dr—dress, drum
fl—flag, flower
fr—frog, fruit
gl—glass, globe
gr—grass, grapes
pl—plug, plant
sk—skunk, skirt
sl—slide, slippers
sm—smile, smoke

sn—snake, snowman
sp—spider, spoon
st—stove, star
sw—swing, swan
tr—triangle, truck

Beginning Consonant Digraphs

sh—shell, shovel, shirt, shark, shoe
th—thermometer, theater, thimble, thirteen, thumb
ch—cherries, chimney, chopsticks, church, checkers
wh—wheat, whale, whistle, whiskers, wheel

Ending Consonants

b—tub, web, crab, crib
ck—duck, truck, clock, stick
d—bird, toad, cloud, sled
f—leaf, roof
g—leg, pig, dog, bag
l—seal, ball, nail
m—broom, jam, arm, drum
n—queen, fun, van, moon
p—clap, snap, cap, stamp
r—paper, zipper, jar
s—prunes, glasses, pants
t—rabbit, tent, puppet, net
v—five, hive
x—ax, six, box

Short Vowels

a—bag, bat, fan, cat, pan, mat, ladder, map, mask, rat

e—vest, nest, desk, eggs, hen, chest, pen, cent, pet

i—lick, dish, fish, chin, lip, pig, pin, six, hill

o—box, log, doll, hop, lock, mop, pot, rock, sock, top

u—bug, bus, cup, duck, gum, cut, nut, run, sun, tub

Long Vowels

a—cake, snail, cage, tail, tape, paint, nail, plate, table, rake

e—sheep, street, bee, needle, tea, teeth, knee, cheek, pea, three, leaf

i—kite, bride, pie, ice, fire, night, tiger, bike, tie, nine

o—goat, hose, cone, rope, soap, toe, toast, bone, throne, boat, nose

u—ruler, mule, fruit, glue, cube, flute

Rhyming Words

hat—cat
stamp—lamp
paw—saw
can—man
ten—hen
bell—well
wig—pig
chick—stick
rock—clock
box—fox
dog—frog
bun—sun
rug—bug
corn—horn

zoo—shoe
cap—map
moon—spoon
train—rain
chair—bear
gate—skate
bed—sled
pop—stop
bib—crib
dice—mice
bride—slide
king—ring
tree—key
kitten—mitten
cry—eye
mouse—house

Syllables

One syllable—seal, bat, kite, hand, bed, ball, cloud, drum, bus

Two syllables—dolphin, balloon, pencil, basket, football, zebra, pumpkin, apple, rainbow

Three syllables—umbrella, strawberry, computer, kangaroo, butterfly, elephant, banana, pineapple, hamburger

Four syllables—helicopter, harmonica, rhinoceros, thermometer, caterpillar, watermelon, television, elevator, motorcycle

2-Column Sorting Mat

3-Column Sorting Mat

4-Column Sorting Mat

5-Column Sorting Mat

Alternative Activities

Memory Match

Choose a picture sort category. Have children spread the picture cards facedown on the table. Invite one child at a time to turn over two separate cards and say the name of the pictures. If the two cards match the same phonics skill or pattern (e.g., rhyming words, beginning consonant sounds), the child who turned them over keeps the cards. If the cards are not a match, the child turns the cards

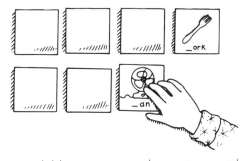

facedown and returns them to the same spot. Encourage children to repeat these steps until all the cards have been matched. Then, have each child count how many matches he or she discovered. The child with the most matches wins the game.

Go Fish!

Divide the class into groups of four. Choose a picture sort category (e.g., short vowels) for each group. (It can be the same category for all groups or different categories for children to rotate groups.) Each child in the group is given four cards and the remaining cards are placed in a center pile. Invite one child at a time to ask another child for a card that would match the sound of a card in his or her hand. For example, a child may say *Do you have a picture with /b/ for the beginning sound?* If the other child has a matching card, he or she gives it to the child who asked to complete a matching pair. If the child does not have a matching card, he or she says *Go Fish!* Then, the child who asked for the card would pick a card from the center pile. Encourage children to repeat these steps until all of the cards have been matched.

Tic-Tac-Toe

Make several copies of the Tic-Tac-Toe reproducible (page 16) on construction paper. Laminate the pages for durability. Divide the class into pairs. Choose a picture sort category, and give one set of picture cards and a Tic-Tac-Toe reproducible to each pair. Have children spread the cards facedown on the table. Invite one child at a time to pick a card, say the name of the picture, and then

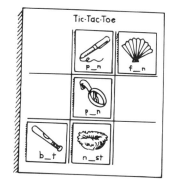

place it on one of the tic-tac-toe squares. Each child must stick to one phonics rule to be able to place a card. For example, a pair of children using the cards for the short vowel picture sort may have one child try to get tic-tac-toe using short *a* pictures (e.g., pan, bat, fan), while his or her partner tries to get tic-tac-toe with short *e* pictures (e.g., nest, hen, pen).

Bingo

Copy nine picture cards onto one sheet of paper to create a Bingo game board. Rearrange the same nine picture cards, and copy them onto a sheet of paper to create additional Bingo game boards. Give each child a Bingo game board and a handful of markers. Hold up a picture card. Have children look at the picture card and then check their Bingo game board for a matching picture card. Invite children to place a marker on their game board if they have a match. Use Bingo to introduce the picture cards of a particular sort or as a review after children have studied a sort category.

Rap with Rhyming Words

Choose a picture sort category, and list the phonics rules for that category on chart or butcher paper. Hang the paper on the wall. Brainstorm with children a variety of words for each column, and write them on the paper. Then, as a whole class or in small groups create a rap using rhyming words from the chart paper. Decide with children on a beat or rhythm for the rap, and practice reading the rap aloud. Invite individual children or small groups to perform the rap for the rest of the class.

I'm Thinking Of . . .

Give each child in a small group 5–8 picture sort cards from one sort category (e.g., ending consonants). Say a clue such as *I'm thinking of a picture that ends in the sound /r/.* Have children look at their picture cards. If a child has a card that matches the statement (e.g., zipper), invite him or her to hold up the card, say the name of the picture aloud, and hand the card to you. Repeat these steps with a variety of different clues until you have collected all the cards.

Act It Out

Choose a picture sort category, and have a volunteer select one of the cards. Have the volunteer act out the word for the other children to guess. Have the child who correctly guesses repeat the process of acting out another picture card.

Sand Writing

Fill the bottom of a cookie sheet with sand. Place a set of ending consonant cards or short vowel cards faceup on the table. Have each child choose a card, spell the word in the sand using his or her finger, and then say it aloud. After children have had practice writing the words in the sand, have them sort the words by pattern and write all of the words for a particular word pattern in the sand.

Beginning Sounds Book

Give each pair of children a large blank sheet of paper. Have each pair pick a beginning consonant letter card. Ask pairs to draw pictures of items that start with the letter on their card. For example, the pair that chooses the B card may draw a ball, banana, bed, broom, and butterfly. Help children label each picture. Combine all the papers to create a Beginning Sounds book.

Tic-Tac-Toe

Beginning Consonants

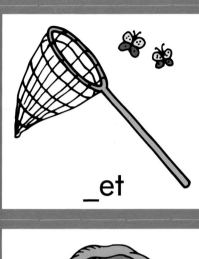

_et

_arachute

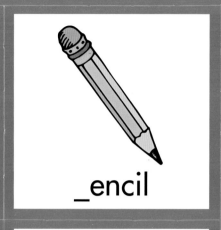

_encil

_izza

_uilt

_uestion mark

_obot

_ainbow

_cissors

_even

_elephone

_urtle

Beginning Consonants

_ase

_acuum

_iolin

_atch

_indow

_-ray

_o-yo

_arn

_awn

_ebra

_oo

_ero

Beginning Consonant Blends

__ock

__anket

__ead

__ush

__othes

__own

__own

__ayon

__ess

__um

__ag

__ower

Beginning Consonant Blends

__og

__uit

__ass

__obe

__ass

__apes

__ug

__ant

__unk

__irt

__ide

__ippers

Beginning Consonant Blends

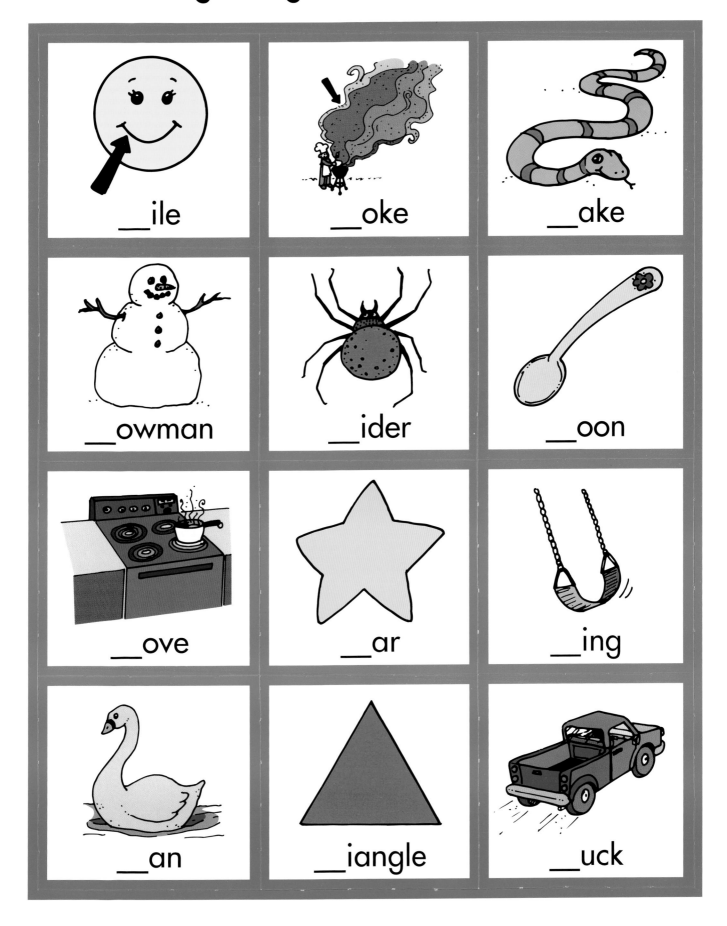

__ile

__oke

__ake

__owman

__ider

__oon

__ove

__ar

__ing

__an

__iangle

__uck

Beginning Consonant Digraphs

Beginning Consonant Digraphs

Ending Consonants

tu__

we__

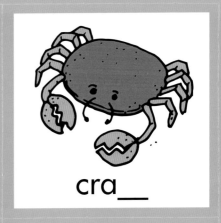

cra__

du__

tru__

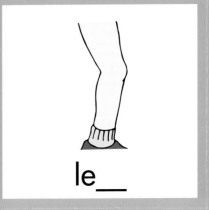

le__

bir__

toa__

lea__

roo__

pi__

do__

Ending Consonants

sea__

bal__

nai__

broo__

ja__

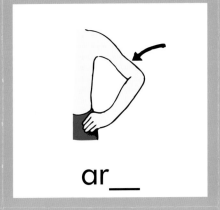

ar__

quee__

fu__

va__

cla__

sna__

pape__

Ending Consonants

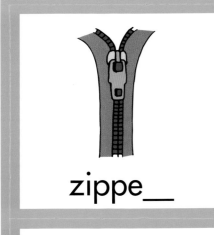

zippe___

ja___

prune___

glasse___

pant___

rabbi___

ten___

puppe___

fi ___e

hi___e

a___

si___

Ending Consonants

ca____

bo____

sti____

moo____

sle____

ba____

stam____

cri____

dru____

clou____

clo____

ne____

Short Vowels

b __ g

b __ t

f __ n

c __ t

p __ n

m __ t

l __ dder

m __ p

m __ sk

r __ t

v __ st

n __ st

Short Vowels

d__sk

__ggs

h__n

ch__st

p__n

c__nt

p__t

l__ck

d__sh

f__sh

ch__n

l__p

Short Vowels

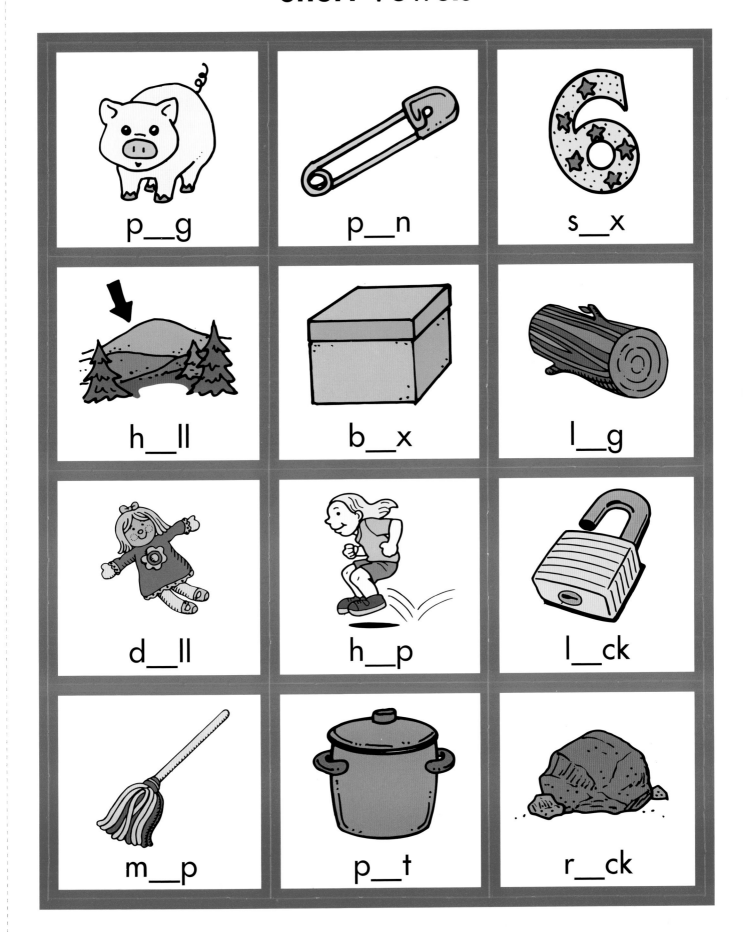

p__g

p__n

s__x

h__ll

b__x

l__g

d__ll

h__p

l__ck

m__p

p__t

r__ck

Short Vowels

s__ck

t__p

b__g

b__s

c__p

d__ck

g__m

c__t

n__t

r__n

s__n

t__b

Long Vowels

c__ke

sn___l

c__ge

t__l

t_pe

p__nt

n___l

pl__te

t__ble

r__ke

str___t

b___

Long Vowels

n___dle

t___

t___th

kn___

ch___k

p___

thr___

l___f

sh___p

p___

___ce

f__re

Long Vowels

br__de

t__ger

b__ke

t___

n__ne

k__te

n__ght

c__ne

h__se

r__pe

s__p

t___

Long Vowels

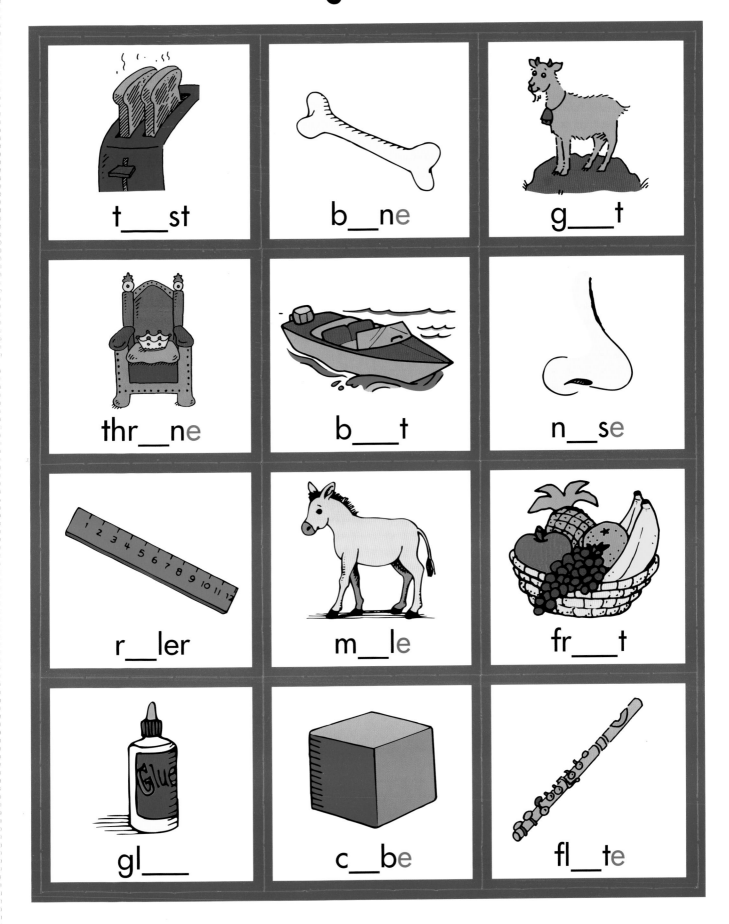

t___st

b__ne

g___t

thr__ne

b___t

n__se

r__ler

m__le

fr___t

gl___

c__be

fl__te

Rhyming Words

Rhyming Words

Rhyming Words

Rhyming Words

Rhyming Words

Syllables

Syllables

Syllables

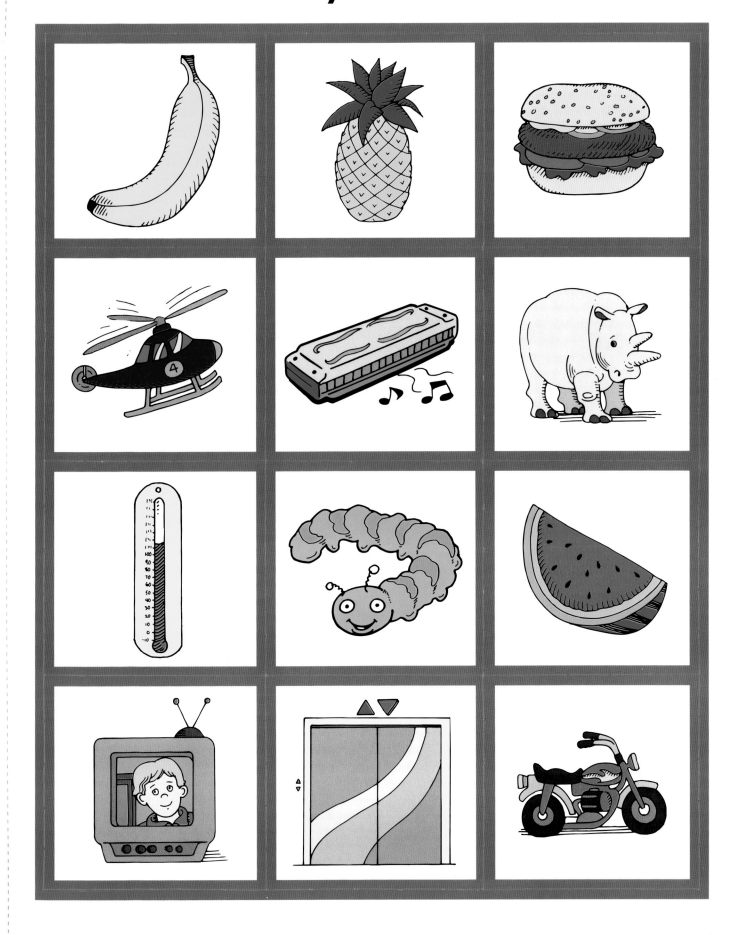

Beginning Consonant Letter Cards

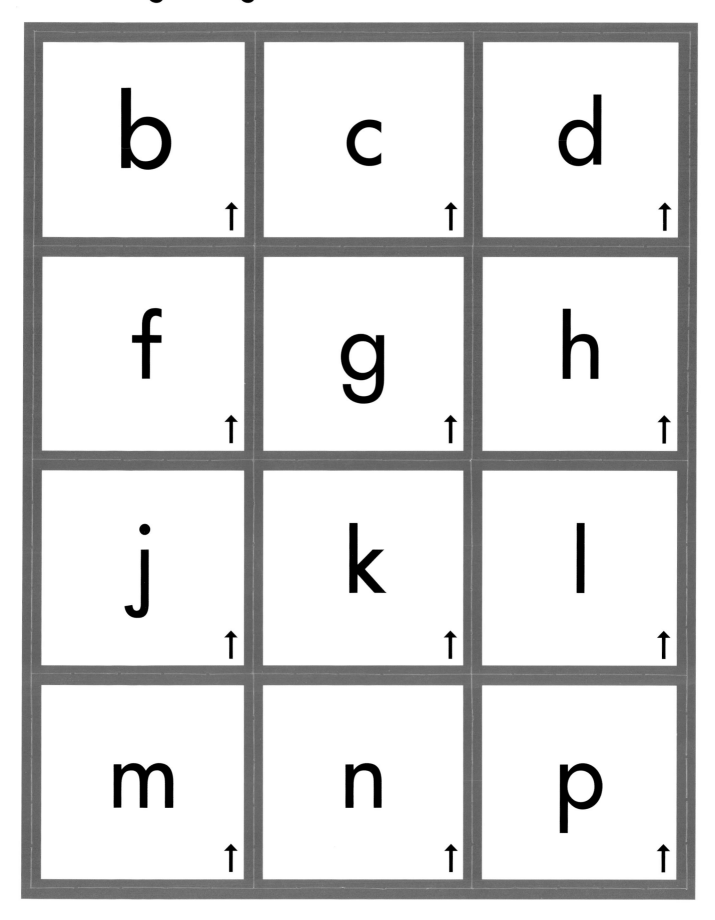

Beginning Consonant Letter Cards

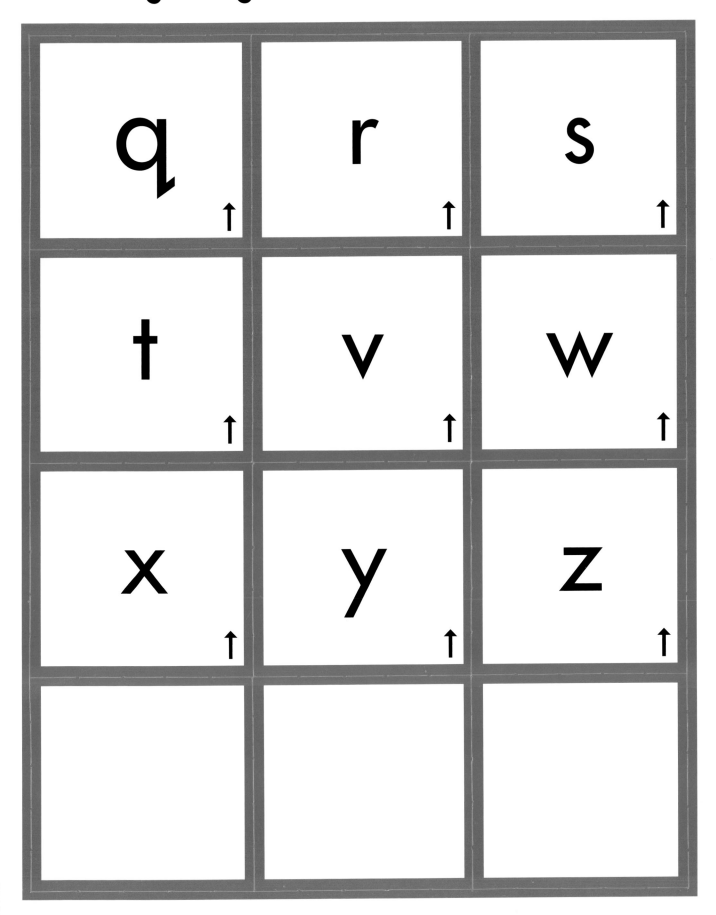

Beginning Consonant Blend Labels

bl	br	cl
cr	dr	fl
pl	fr	gl
gr	sk	sl
sm	sn	sp
st	sw	tr

Ending Consonant Labels

b ↑	ck ↑	d ↑
f ↑	g ↑	l ↑
m ↑	n ↑	p ↑
r ↑	s ↑	t ↑
v ↑	x ↑	

Vowels and Syllables Labels

long ā	long ē	long ī
long ō	long ū	short ă
short ĕ	short ĭ	short ŏ
short ŭ		
		1 syllable
2 syllables	3 syllables	4 syllables